MELODIES FROM HEAVEN

MELODIES FROM HEAVEN

BAILEY MARIE

J. Merrill
PUBLISHING

J Merrill Publishing, Inc., Columbus 43207
www.JMerrill.pub

Library of Congress Control Number: 2020925071
ISBN-13: 978-1-950719-74-7 (Paperback)
ISBN-13: 978-1-950719-73-0 (eBook)

Title: Melodies from Heaven
Author: Bailey Marie

CONTENTS

1. Clearing the Air — 1

2. When God Speaks — 3

3. History — 7

4. Simon of Cyrene — 9

5. Two-Faced — 13

6. Anything and Everything — 17

7. A Letter I Penned to Myself — 19

8. Dry Bones — 23

9. Kill Joy — 25

10. You Are Living — 29

11. At Capacity — 33

12. For the Dreamer in You — 37

13. Altar Call — 41

14. Martyr — 45

About Bailey — 47

CLEARING THE AIR

This is the last call for everything foul
to leave voluntarily NOW.

Foolish is the demon that taunts me.
I change the air space when I walk into any place.

I command angels in this moment
to play red rover
with the spirits that taunt you.
I speak to the original opinion of you.
The silhouette,
The image of you.

I say...
that you are royalty.
And you shall conduct yourselves accordingly.
I dismantle every attack from the enemy.
I silence every voice that speaks in an attempt to sound
like God.
YOU ARE NOT.

I command every excursion of perversion to CEASE.
I declare that the key to your salvation be released.
I pray while you're in my space,
that Yeshua gets to do everything he's longed to.
And that he deposits the same revelations he's placed in me,
in you.

I decree that it will be infectious
& transfer to every soul you come into contact with.
And at the appointed hour may it manifest.

Until then, let it be safely kept
from all harm
& and prying ears that seek to destroy you.
May life be connected to you at the hip
& death avoid you.

I draw your purpose to you.
Kingdom come & will be done through you.

In Yeshua's name, we count this done.

Welcome.
You belong to the kingdom.

WHEN GOD SPEAKS

This one's for the people who Yeshua has never spoken to.
This one is for the people who sat in that church pew and felt
like the preacher had a word for everybody, BUT you.

This is for everyone who has walked
into a church and felt looked down on.
Like they forgot, Yeshua died for the remission of our sins.
They took those thorns off his head
and made YOU put the crown on.

You were never meant to be crucified like the Messiah.
Just like the church was never meant to be filled with
judgmental hypocrites and bold-faced liars.

I'm sorry, that someone has either
over exaggerated or diluted the truth.

But before you treat me like a Jehovah's Witness and close
the door, there are 3 things GOD would like to say to you;

(1)

You were made in my image,
but you were never meant to BE me.
So, the next time you walk in a church,
know that I was pierced in my side
for every side-eye you receive.

(2)

When people tell you not to believe in ME... stop them.
It's not a coincidence that
Buddha, Allah, Oshun & King Tut are okay, but me?
I'm a problem.

Don't let them tell you that I was savior of the KKK
and pushed on you when you were slaves.
Look, you all believe you're good people, right?

Well, it's no different than someone robbing a bank
then giving authorities your name.
This is just one of the many times that I've been framed.

But be not mistaken,
I am he ... who was, is, and is to come
after that, there is no conversation starter;
the conversation is done.

(3)

The lack of Godliness in others
should not determine what YOU do.
So long as you walk this earth,
there will be an opposing force that desires to shift you.

You are meant to be fortified in my presence.
Where I speak to you freely,

and you're surrounded by my essence.

OH! AND ONE MORE THING!

(4)

Those who truly represent me do not wear
the garments of hypocrites and liars.
The devil dresses in deceit... the blood of Yeshua?
Is designer.

SEE THIS ONE
is for the ones whom I have never spoken to.
Lift your head, be not dismayed because
I... just spoke to you.

HISTORY

God change my name like Saul.
Erase every trace of who I used to be,
like Paul.

So that when those who knew me
run down their list of broken laws,

they get to my name
They can't find anything at all.

Forgive me for my habitual requests for a renewing.
I command my spirit to be in remembrance
of the promise that HE will do a new thing.

Every wildfire in my life,
your blood has smothered,
It covers,
more than that of a nurturing church mother.

Sticks and stones could never break my bones.
It couldn't stop the rising of the Messiah.

And if I be his child, it won't stop me either.

SIMON OF CYRENE

If we think about why most black people,
young and old, don't want to be Christians.
I believe it's because we've adopted this philosophy that we
all derived from Pharaohs and queens of the Egyptians.

Instead of looking to the truth of
what is part of our origin.
For instance, a former city in Libya called Cyrene.

Also known, to have had been home
to a black man named Simon.

See this black man named Simon
had been given a very crucial assignment.

As Yeshua walked with his cross, physically weak.
As blood dripped down his bronze colored cheeks,
Simon was passing through.
Probably minding his business as us black folks often do.

But then Simon of Cyrene,
who happened to come upon this gruesome scene,
was pressed by the Romans to aid the human manifestation
of Jehovah Jireh.
This black man Simon upon his back,
carried the cross meant to crucify the Messiah.

You see, I took this as a sign,
better yet, a confirmation of our assignment.
This black man Simon
put all of us into alignment.

This last war cry that will set the captives free
will come through the black community.

And, of course, the enemy doesn't like it.
Wanna know the reason
for this huge black people identity crisis?
So when God calls your name, you won't recognize it.

We struggle to pass through
cause these roaming men in blue are
pressing us to carry these false charges.

And we do it.

Only this time around,
they're not wooden, they're silver bullets.
You believe in these Pharaohs because they led you to it.

Foolish of you to think it was you who chooses.
These Pharaohs ordered for your execution.

Still don't believe me?

Look at the present-day remains of the birthplace of Simon.
Black people who are not slain,
are a part of the slave trade in Libya.

Black men are being sold at auctions for 400 dollars.
Worldly philosophy says history will repeat itself.
God said my people will perish for their lack of knowledge.

I hope you all are taking notes.
Just cause the all-seeing eye is an open eye
It doesn't mean you "woke."

If Jesus was a trick of the white man,
then I'm sure our ancestors would've let us know.
My great, great, great grandmother didn't pray to an Egyptian
god, and she didn't burn no sage smoke.

I'm sure that on Sundays,
she snuck and sat with the reading slaves.

As they told the parts of the Bible that masta left out.
I'm just trying to figure out why we have yet to realize
and fully accept the truth they figured out.

We are a great part of history.

And if the woman with the issue of blood
was blessed for touching Yeshua's garment,

Simon carried the cross
ask yourself, "what does that mean for me."

Please do yourself and the kingdom a favor
and take a true interest in your history.

Don't get lost in being black,
But rather connect with it biblically.

TWO-FACED

"And He said to them, "Go into all the world and preach the
gospel to all creation."
Mark 16:15

Some of you won't minister outside
of the four walls where your church is stationed.
Never thought I'd see the day when the saved
still needed saving.

And then condemn the ones in the world who drown.
Looking to be captains in the church,
but you left no life rafts around.
Praying for mercy on souls AFTER
their bodies are in the ground.

Oh, but you're Christ-like,
You talk so much mess about the people you worship with,
That the lost see you and don't like Christ.

Let me put it this way.

Pretend it's just you and me,
With a table full of food to eat.
You've never had it, so you tell me to try it.

And despite the fact that my mouth is speaking its praise,
I scrunch up my face
indicating that I didn't like it.

Now by looking at me,
why would you want to taste and see, that the lord is good?
Seeing as how my life does not mirror my gratitude
towards God as it should.

Why is it that we act like Yeshua
was to be the only example of how Great God is?
Examine your image, evict foul spirit tenants,
and tell them this temple is where God lives.

And then Live it.
When people come and ask you for directions
to the way, the truth and the light,
show them, don't give it.

Know that some people will only come
to challenge your faith as if it is theory.
Clothe yourself in the armor of God,
Respond with word and not feeling.

Ya know
I feel as though when life's credits roll
the question of judgment will not be who has the purest soul.

But I feel like God will ask me
Bailey, how many seats do you need?

I want to be able to say I brought a million
souls to the kingdom with me.

I want to be able to say God's Glory on me was like a
lighthouse that radiates, drawing people from all over near.
Like God, I did what you said,
snatched souls out of hell, and brought them here.

This is the Goal in the kingdom.
Our brothers and sisters are shackled.
WE must free them.
If not you, then who?

These souls are our assignment.
I hear God saying, I dispatch you
the way you dispatch angels.

Now go out and find them.
Kingdom will come
And his will be done
Through you.

Each and every one of you have souls
that you're assigned to.
Your disobedience has nothing to do with you
and everything to do with the person you're attached to.

Realize,
that I am not talking about intercourse
when I am discussing soul ties.

God created your destiny to fulfill a need.
So like all the other times I'll say my favorite line
Manifest. Be.

ANYTHING AND EVERYTHING

He never said it would be easy to be a believer.
And yet, most of us are ready to quit God like a bad habit
when we see blessings raining,
and WE are not the receiver.

See, that's just it.
Sometimes the test of faith is to see
if you'll break over the things
that you don't get.

To see if you are still child-like in your walk with Christ.
Or if you've REALLY surrendered your life to him.
Are you willing to give up anything and everything to gain
anything and everything that he has for you?

Or are you gonna spend the next year in fear
just to end up standing back here
Listening to the same message about what God's gonna do?

Look to your neighbor,

and with all of God's favor,
Tell their opposition
"Loose here!"

And if they still don't wanna walk
after God knocked them chains off,

well… you shouldn't have known
because you should've been gone
and not left there.

Because YOU said that you were willing
to do anything and everything to gain anything
and everything that God has for you.

So, what are you waiting for?
You heard the call.

Move.

A LETTER I PENNED TO MYSELF

You've always wanted this...
But your reasoning has changed.

When did you get so angry? So bitter?
When did you fill up on promises?
When did you go empty?

You just want to prove a point.
Prove that you're valuable.
You just want to be the first pick
instead of the runt of the litter.

You just want justice.
You want all to be fair.

But nothing is fair in love n war.
You chose war.

You're a martyr.

You picked the door you're walking through.
You'll always feel shortchanged.

Alienated.

People will always reap what YOU sow.
Because you chose that.
Why do you keep searching for a pat on the back? Don't you
know you have two hands?

You will never be good enough for them.
You will never find confidence in a standing ovation.

You know.
You've had plenty of them.
This is the last place you play the victim.

You know if you just do it, you'll fly.
Stop waiting for people to board the plane.
This road is lonely,
Bailey, you knew that.

You are loved.

Just not in the way that you want it.
Rewards are given once you've done your job.
You won't even interview.
Quit taking internships with your gift.

Dance.
Sing.
Rap.
Recite.
Act.

With everything in you.
Bleed for it for once.

Don't be afraid.
Don't be ashamed.
Don't be embarrassed.

For a place has been prepared for you
And only you.

I love you.
So, you should, too.

Go.

DRY BONES

A walk in my shoes would be a walk to remember.
And if I had to choose my brand of shoes,
it'd be the blood-stained, high top,
queasy till Septembers.

All my life, I felt odd.
Abused sexually, mentally, and spiritually
I still found time to believe in God.

I never seemed to lose my faith...
Until one fateful day, I convinced myself that the wages of sin
was a good enough price to pay.

Trying my best not to die,
I depended on higher than highs,
I preyed on the ganja leaf.

Eyebrow razors left temporary cuts that,
after a while, you can't see.
This is what self-medication has done to me.

Hospital bed and empty pill bottle was the reason why.
Embarrassed at my failed attempt,
I was only regretting one thing...
That I didn't die.

Convincing myself at checkout that I'd
wait another few months to try.
Driving to Drizzy,
dizzy,
I had no lust for life.

Then something told me I needed to be born again.

Because babies after birth,
all they want to do is get the chance to breathe in.
So, I moved to an airspace that I thought was safe, and I
breathed in.

I breathed in... Everything BUT oxygen.
Shamelessly drinking out of glasses labeled sin
because no one had a problem openly speaking
about this vessel my spirit lives in.

I fed, thinking hopefully,
my gluttony would lead me to death.
Telling God to send me home.
I didn't care if he wasn't finished yet.

I know,
You're waiting for the part about regret.
You're waiting for the part where I forgive but don't forget.

I could, I would, I probably should.
But... I'm not there yet.

KILL JOY

I could see myself with you... forever.

And baby, what I do, I do well
& no one can do it better see...

I could see myself with you...
Forever.

So, don't think it strange when your man or lady explains that
I'm the reason y'all could never be together see...

They're way too tired of
your late-night rendezvous with me...
Exploring parts of your psyche that they have never...
Will never... See.

Causing downright, straight up, jealousy.
And when they hear lyrics like,
"Ain't nothin' I won't do for you..."
They think of you and me.

I got you pill poppin' after these threesomes with anxiety.
Got you on Facebook, Twitter, and Instagram
posting memes like,

"You know that's bae when bae start using your slang."
I got you walking, talking, and looking like me,
but you still won't claim my name.

I am the lesson that'll have you questioning life.
I am the illness that will have you
not eating, sleeping, or thinking right.

I'm worse than the boyfriend that beats you
and buys you MAC so you can still look good.

I step to the bridge you call faith used to reach
your hopes and dreams and say,
Nigga, I wish you WOULD...

Move.

I've plagued minds for generations.
What makes you think I won't plague you?

Everything could be going right,
and I'll still show up in the middle of the night
for no other reason except I felt like it.

And at first, you'll try to convince
yourself that you're okay,
But you'll give way...

I'll be Mayweather &
like Pacquaio, you'll be done fightin'.

And I've got my way like it's destined,
tears running from your face to your chest then...

WAIT!!!!!

I forgot to introduce myself,
the doctors call me depression.
And I come for the sole purpose of
making you feel less than.

That you might end your everlasting life.
And if not, that's alright cause...
Baby, I could see myself with you...
Forever.

And baby what I do,
I do well & no one could do it better

See...

I could see myself in you...

Forever.

YOU ARE LIVING

I was in a place where I believed God didn't reside.
Where religion and my life decisions collide.

Forced into transparency
wearing flashcards stained
with names
for the way they looked at me,

I felt I was no longer made in your image.
But I thank your son's name that you didn't.

You should be proud of the way you raised your baby boy.
How you taught him to love those who,
to the world, may seem unstable.
Kind of like that jock that sits with
a loner kid at the lunch table.

He sat with me,
and when I felt like crying, he laughed with me.

I got mad at him, but he never got mad
and removed his grace from me,
even when I loved him unfaithfully.

My open affairs with self-pity and jealousy,
not understanding why it was always
easy for people to unlove me,

Father, what did I do?
And before I could ask why,
all I read from his weeping eyes was
"daughter, me too."

He said Bailey Marie, we are more alike than you see.
I, too, prayed for people who dare not pray for me.

And you struggling to bare a cross, while your Judas' watch,
is just Satan's attempt to make you experience
your own twisted version of Calvary.
But it cannot be redone, what they did to me.

And my love for you is why I was slain.
So even when you are angry with me,
I won't let them kill you.
Even when he killed Abel, I was STILL God of Cain.

Know that Sometimes favor means loneliness,
and anointing calls for brokenness.
And your enemies will envy your progress
but could not for a day endure the process.

Your forced transparency is by design.
So that when the day comes when I parade you around as you
exalt me,

there will be no question that you are mine.

There is no place that, if I choose to, I cannot reside.
Wipe those tears from your eyes
and see that I CHOOSE to be by your side.

Know that there isn't a concert that
you put on in your mind that I have missed.
There isn't a play that you've envisioned
where I wasn't the first guest on the list.

I love you,
even when you let your mind
take you to dark places, I never quit.
I've kissed - every - slit - wrist.

And at night,
when you wanted to die, I was your life.
All I ask now is that you would give me time.

I just want to talk to you,
let me be who I am,
let me be the God of you.

For I came that you might have life
& that you might have it more abundantly.
You are living, and despite what you may think,
You are doing it wonderfully.

AT CAPACITY

Some people could never understand certain dynamics of love
because they don't have the capacity to love that way.

My love, it was never you.

Stop taking responsibility for altering views that you never
had enough power OR influence to change in the first place.

This blame game should be a sin.

Let's say it is.

So, I rebuke self loathe and pray the blood of Yeshua will
wash away the isolation they doused you in.

My love, you are WORTHY of companionship.

And I pray you find good company.

People who will never have you seeing red, testing your
boundaries.

Because they're by the book
& value staying in the lines like coloring.

People who value honesty.
Basic morals have their loyalty.

Schizophrenic,
when they see you, they see purple,
Royalty.

And if they don't,
give them that quick dismiss.

They put on a great show. Take a bow.
But Tolerate no forms of abuse, baby; they ain't Chris.

The right time to say goodbye is now,
because you ARE worthy.

Worthy of your own love.

You may love them too much
to find a reason to walk away,
But Baby, love YOU enough.

Enough to not make excuses.
Enough to go off instinct and not wait
for somebody else to PROVE it.

Love you enough.
Because you are enough.

Cut all unhealthy,
toxic ties so that when they walk away,
It doesn't trip YOU up.

Because you're finally aware that Some people could never
understand certain dynamics of love.

They just don't have the capacity to love that way.

My love, it was never you.

FOR THE DREAMER IN YOU

Bailey,
You are a dreamer, but don't let that be all that you know.
You were just a babe, but Dr. Seuss was prophesying to you,
"Oh, the places you will go."

I am not a cruel God,
You would not dream it if you could not achieve it.
Do you know why I give man dreams?
Because there are no limitations
on what I can do when you are sleeping.

It's also the time that the enemy creeps,
in a foolish attempt to sound like me.
My promise for you was not designed
to rest in your thoughts.

You and your dreams were meant
to do more than just pillow talk.
Two things cannot occupy the same
space at the same time.

Maybe the vision would remain
if you stop greeting fear and doubt
when you open your eyes.

Bailey,
alone YOU can't.
You're right.
But YOU are not I.

I am that I am,
The original Sandman.
Anything you can't do,
you better believe I CAN.

It can and will happen for you, society lies.
And if you bring your gifts to me,
I promise, room will be made for you
when you open your eyes.

If you believe, praise me,
If you dare, then daydream.

If there be any faith, write out the acceptance speech.
Make the world into believers,
show them what you accomplished while you were asleep.
Show them the true definition of Dream.

To Dream,
the Second definition,
Is to contemplate the possibility of doing
something or that something might be the case.

I want no limits,
no low altitude dimensions,

no ceilings,
I want faith!

Bailey,
You are a dreamer, but don't let that be
all you have to show.

Submit to my will, take that leap of faith
and watch the places that you will go.

ALTAR CALL

It seems like no matter how far I go,
I always come back to you.

You reel me in.

You hold the reigns to my soul, forever reminding me of the
time that I proclaimed it is anchored in you.

So here I am, embarrassed.

Hoping you still receive royalties from these accolades.

Hoping these debts are not too far past due to be paid.

I'm hoping you still love me...
Because if we're being honest,
there were times when I felt like I didn't want you.

And even those times I came home,
I treated temptation like it was an Uber.

I treated repentance like a credit card.

But no matter how many times I swiped, you made sure that
your grace and your mercy never declined.

Oh, who is man that you are mindful of him?

And the son of man that you care for him?

God, why did you decide to still bless me in a service that I
refused to lift my hands in?

How is it that even when camouflaged, you see me?

Took me from a time when my mouth was shut and let me
find worship through poetry.

Oh, who am I that you are mindful of me?

And then you turned this art form into prophecy.

Manifesting every declaration spoken over me.
Molding me into your image.
Making me a literal definition
of your word so that I cannot return to you void.

This feeling of emptiness is your desire to fulfill.

So, I'll stop forwarding these chain letters filled with my sob
stories, and I'll subscribe to your will.

I will not allow the enemy who is stuck in my past to
consume me in your presence.

I'll stop digging up old dirt and leave it where you left it.

Because I understand it is the enemy's desire
to sift me like wheat.

And I'm embarrassed because I gave him credit for it.

That's what I thought was happening when I was weak.

But little did I know.
You were sifting me through my circumstance to gather up
the remnants of Gold.
He says this is the altar call for your soul.

Prodigal Sons and daughters, put on your robes.

And know that there's no place like home.

And if you get lost, then follow that Christ,
blood-stained, red brick road.

Because I need you,
to feed my people
who need me.

You were never meant to follow the trend
of poor me, you were meant for leading.

You know you can move that mountain
in my name, so why are you pleading?

Quit playing tug-o-war with the devil when it comes to your
destiny. Don't you know you're my child?

Like blonde melodies that stick out in the midst of brunette
harmonies, don't you know you stick out?

This red carpet is for you.

I have angels preparing the way in wait for your arrival.

People will marvel in awe under the weight
of your arrival because I will be with you.

There is no circumstance nor any Issue that can bind you.

Because with my power, my love,
and my blood, I have combined you.

I have your peace
your joy
your open door
waiting for you to step into.

But you cannot be who you want to be,
you must be who you are meant to.

We are running out of time, don't you see?

So manifest and be,

Bailey Marie.

MARTYR

As I stand here with a
spiritually busted lip.

A black eye.

A torn heart.

Battered and bruised.

My soul still cries and demands that, by GOD, I be used.

If his Glory was buried under stones,
and the only way to receive it was to suffer
bleeding flesh and broken bones.

Only to feel an OUNCE of Glory
as the remnant of stones fall to the floor.

I'll lift my blood-stained face to the sky
and cry,

My God!!
My God!!
ABBA!!!

I want more...

ABOUT BAILEY

Bailey Marie is a performing spoken word artist born and raised in Columbus, Ohio.

Her passion for ministry and the arts began at a very early age. She was only three years old when her gifting for wordplay was realized, and it has served as an artistic outlet throughout tough periods of her life.

What started as a coping mechanism quickly turned into a hobby and now a profession.

Her goal is to use this art form to encourage, enlighten, and entertain all people regardless of age, race, or religious background.

facebook.com/bailey.marie.10297

CPSIA information can be obtained
at www.ICGtesting.com
Printed in the USA
BVHW071720090321
602118BV00013B/1593